To: _____

Through his presents, may
you experience his presence!

From: _____

Experience God's Christmas Presence
Copyright ©1996 by The Zondervan Corporation
ISBN 0-310-96786-4

Requests for information should be addressed to:

▨ Zondervan Publishing House,
    Grand Rapids, Michigan 49530

Project Editor: Joy L. Marple
Creative Manager: Patricia Matthews
Graphic Designer: Mark Veldheer
Illustrations: Robin Moro

EXPERIENCE

God's

CHRISTMAS

Presence™

Zondervan Publishing House

Grand Rapids, Michigan

A Division of HarperCollinsPublishers

May all your
dreams be based on
the belief that they
can be reached…

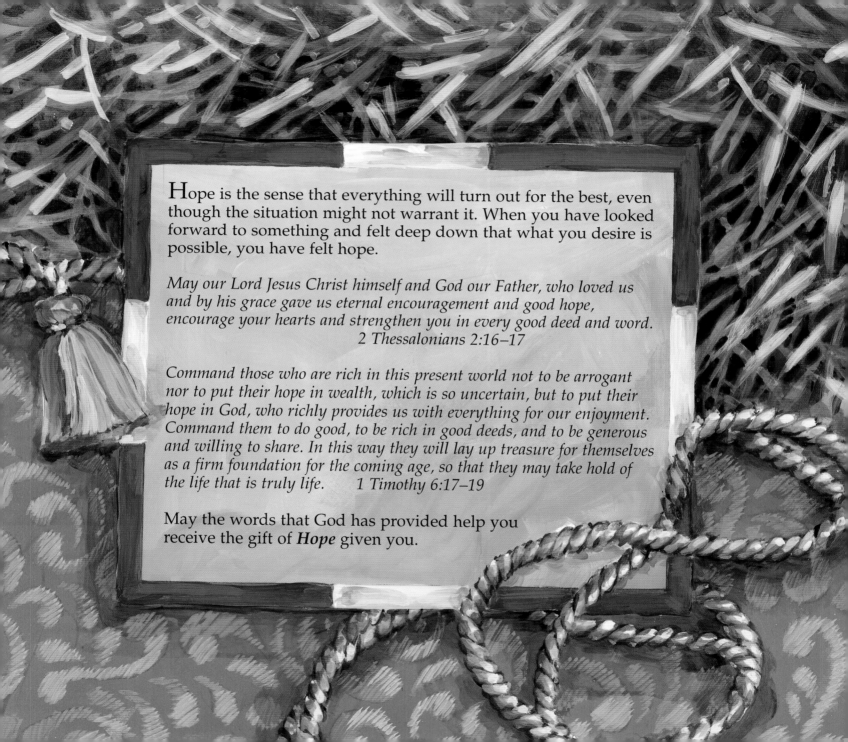

Hope is the sense that everything will turn out for the best, even though the situation might not warrant it. When you have looked forward to something and felt deep down that what you desire is possible, you have felt hope.

May our Lord Jesus Christ himself and God our Father, who loved us and by his grace gave us eternal encouragement and good hope, encourage your hearts and strengthen you in every good deed and word.
2 Thessalonians 2:16–17

Command those who are rich in this present world not to be arrogant nor to put their hope in wealth, which is so uncertain, but to put their hope in God, who richly provides us with everything for our enjoyment. Command them to do good, to be rich in good deeds, and to be generous and willing to share. In this way they will lay up treasure for themselves as a firm foundation for the coming age, so that they may take hold of the life that is truly life. 1 Timothy 6:17–19

May the words that God has provided help you receive the gift of **Hope** given you.

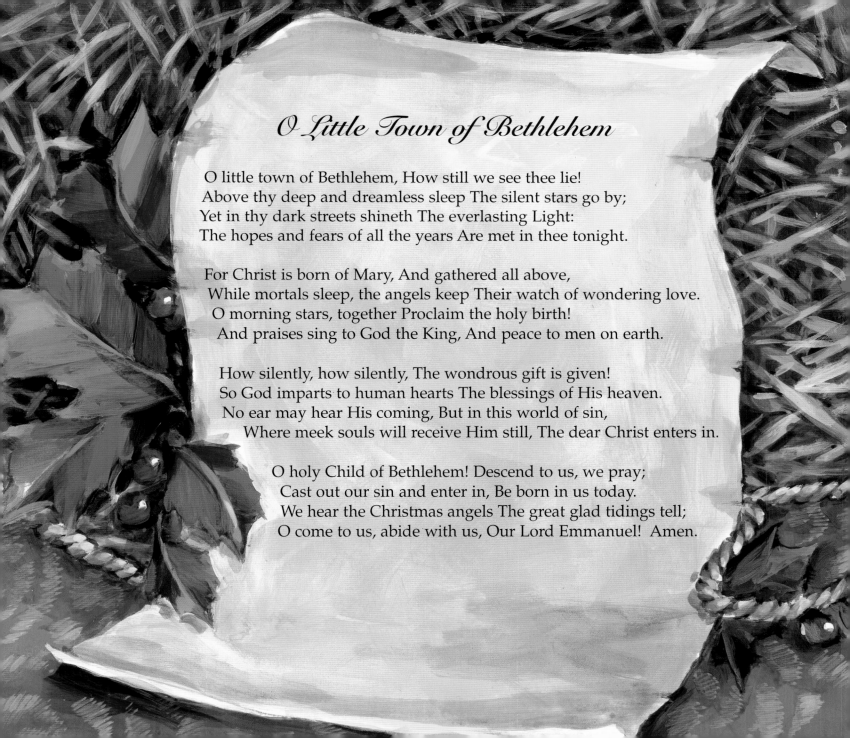

O Little Town of Bethlehem

O little town of Bethlehem, How still we see thee lie!
Above thy deep and dreamless sleep The silent stars go by;
Yet in thy dark streets shineth The everlasting Light:
The hopes and fears of all the years Are met in thee tonight.

For Christ is born of Mary, And gathered all above,
While mortals sleep, the angels keep Their watch of wondering love.
O morning stars, together Proclaim the holy birth!
And praises sing to God the King, And peace to men on earth.

How silently, how silently, The wondrous gift is given!
So God imparts to human hearts The blessings of His heaven.
No ear may hear His coming, But in this world of sin,
Where meek souls will receive Him still, The dear Christ enters in.

O holy Child of Bethlehem! Descend to us, we pray;
Cast out our sin and enter in, Be born in us today.
We hear the Christmas angels The great glad tidings tell;
O come to us, abide with us, Our Lord Emmanuel! Amen.

May quietness and tranquility fill you with a sense of everlasting safety and security...

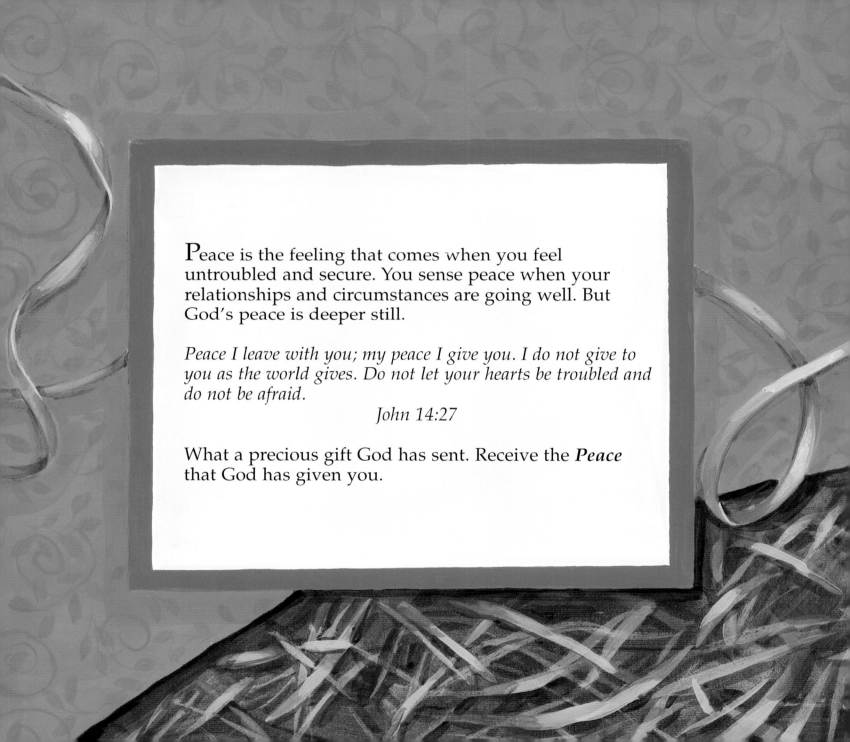

Peace is the feeling that comes when you feel untroubled and secure. You sense peace when your relationships and circumstances are going well. But God's peace is deeper still.

Peace I leave with you; my peace I give you. I do not give to you as the world gives. Do not let your hearts be troubled and do not be afraid.

John 14:27

What a precious gift God has sent. Receive the **Peace** that God has given you.

It Came upon the Midnight Clear

It came upon the midnight clear, That glorious song of old,
From angels bending near the earth To touch their harps of gold:
"Peace on the earth, goodwill to men, From heaven's all
   gracious King":
The world in solemn stillness lay To hear the angels sing.

And ye, beneath life's crushing load, Whose forms are bending low,
Who toil along the climbing way With painful steps and slow,
Look now! for glad and golden hours Come swiftly on the
wing:
O rest beside the weary load, And hear the angels sing.

For lo, the days are hastening on, By prophet seen of old,
When, with the ever circling years, Shall come the time foretold,
When the new heaven and earth shall own The Prince of Peace
   their King,
And the whole world send back the song Which now the
   angels sing.

May divine strength
and encouragement
give you freedom from
trouble and worry…

For You

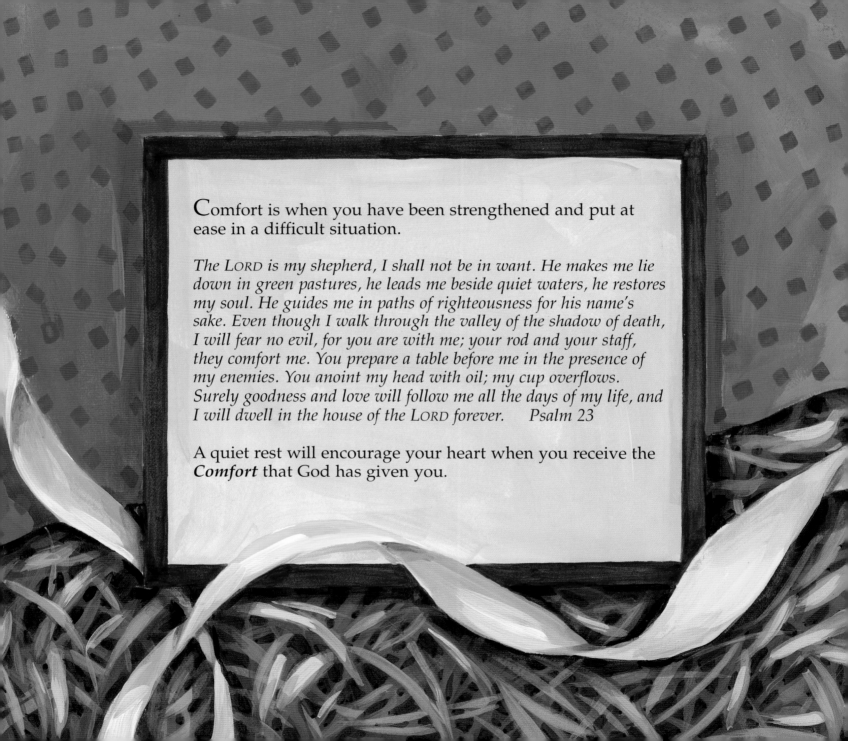

Comfort is when you have been strengthened and put at ease in a difficult situation.

The LORD is my shepherd, I shall not be in want. He makes me lie down in green pastures, he leads me beside quiet waters, he restores my soul. He guides me in paths of righteousness for his name's sake. Even though I walk through the valley of the shadow of death, I will fear no evil, for you are with me; your rod and your staff, they comfort me. You prepare a table before me in the presence of my enemies. You anoint my head with oil; my cup overflows. Surely goodness and love will follow me all the days of my life, and I will dwell in the house of the LORD forever. Psalm 23

A quiet rest will encourage your heart when you receive the ***Comfort*** that God has given you.

God Rest You Merry, Gentlemen

God rest you merry, gentlemen, Let nothing you dismay,
Remember Christ our Saviour Was born on Christmas Day,
To save us all from Satan's pow'r When we were gone astray;

From God our Heavenly Father, A blessed Angel came;
And unto certain Shepherds Bro't tidings of the same:
How that in Bethlehem was born The Son of God by Name.

"Fear not then," said the Angel, "Let nothing you affright,
This day is born a Saviour Of a pure Virgin bright,
To free all those who trust in Him From Satan's pow'r and might."

The shepherds at those tidings Rejoiced much in mind,
And left their flocks afeeding, In tempest, storm, and wind:
And went to Bethlehem straightway, The Son of God to find.

And when they came to Bethlehem Where our dear Saviour lay,
They found Him in a manger, Where oxen feed on hay;
His Mother Mary kneeling down, Unto the Lord did pray.

Chorus:
O tidings of comfort and joy, comfort and joy,
O tidings of comfort and joy.

Allow this gift to fill you with the delight of true happiness...

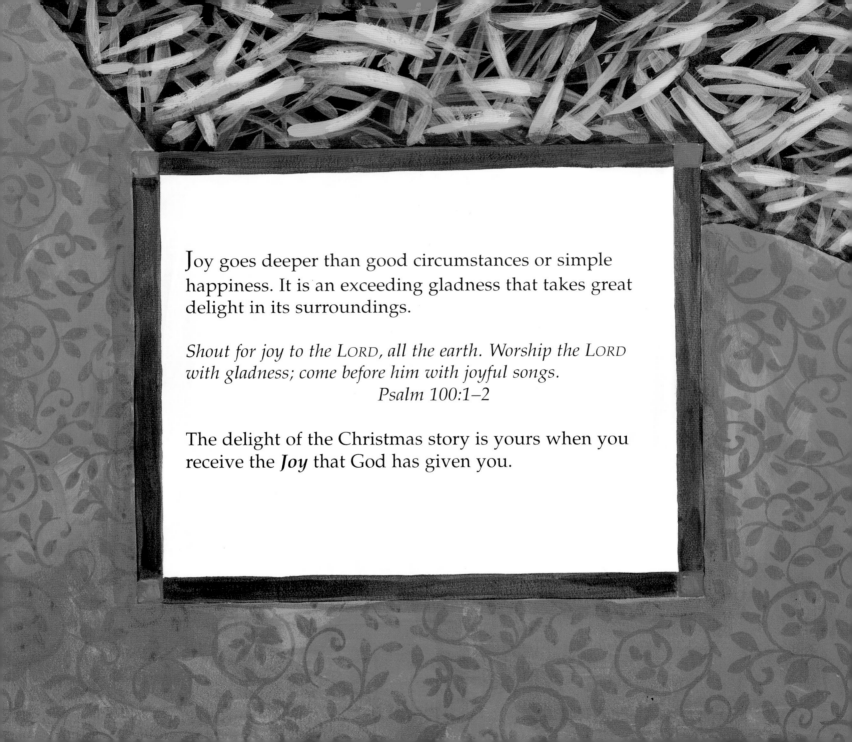

Joy goes deeper than good circumstances or simple happiness. It is an exceeding gladness that takes great delight in its surroundings.

Shout for joy to the LORD, all the earth. Worship the LORD with gladness; come before him with joyful songs.
Psalm 100:1–2

The delight of the Christmas story is yours when you receive the **Joy** that God has given you.

Joy to the World!

Joy to the world! the Lord is come:
Let earth receive her King;
Let every heart prepare Him room,
And heaven and nature sing,
And heaven and nature sing,
And heaven, and heaven and nature sing.

Joy to the world! the Savior reigns:
Let men their songs employ;
While fields and floods, rocks, hills, and plains
Repeat the sounding joy,
Repeat the sounding joy,
Repeat, repeat the sounding joy.

No more let sins and sorrows grow,
Nor thorns infest the ground;
He comes to make His blessings flow
Far as the curse is found,
Far as the curse is found,
Far as, far as the curse is found.

He rules the world with truth and grace,
And makes the nations prove
The glories of His righteousness,
And wonders of His love,
And wonders of His love,
And wonders, wonders of His love. Amen.

For You

Love is a warm and caring affection that is felt for another person. However, God's love is unconditional, given to us freely regardless of our words, thoughts or actions.

Dear friends, let us love one another, for love comes from God. Everyone who loves has been born of God and knows God. Whoever does not love does not know God, because God is love. This is how God showed his love among us: He sent his one and only Son into the world that we might live through him. This is love: not that we loved God, but that he loved us and sent his Son as an atoning sacrifice for our sins. Dear friends, since God so loved us, we also ought to love one another.

1 John 4:7–11

Receive the *Love* that God has given you through this tiny child in a lowly manger.

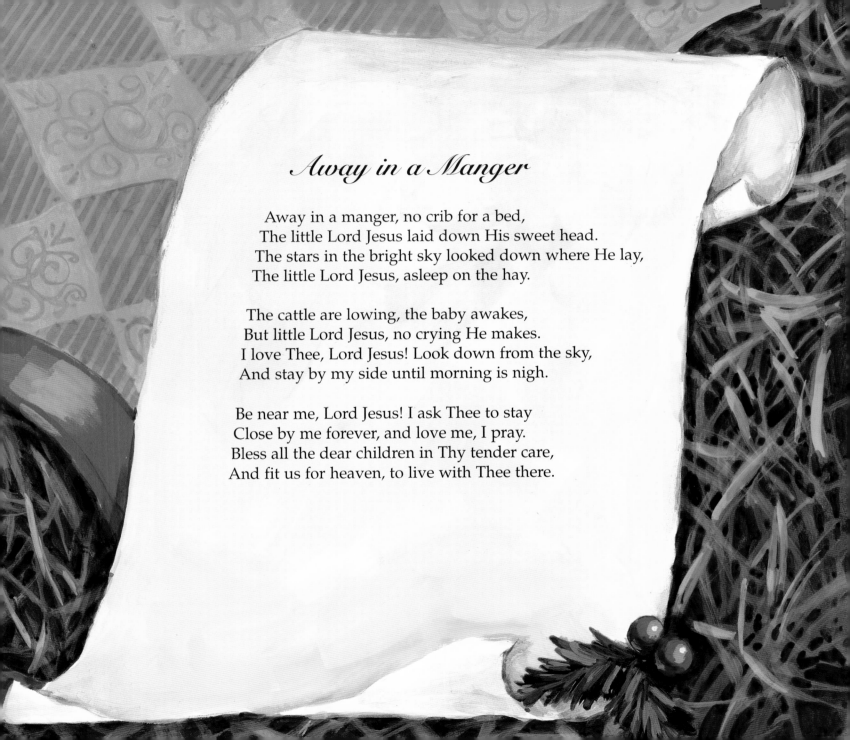

Away in a Manger

Away in a manger, no crib for a bed,
The little Lord Jesus laid down His sweet head.
The stars in the bright sky looked down where He lay,
The little Lord Jesus, asleep on the hay.

The cattle are lowing, the baby awakes,
But little Lord Jesus, no crying He makes.
I love Thee, Lord Jesus! Look down from the sky,
And stay by my side until morning is nigh.

Be near me, Lord Jesus! I ask Thee to stay
Close by me forever, and love me, I pray.
Bless all the dear children in Thy tender care,
And fit us for heaven, to live with Thee there.

Faith is a belief that is not based on visible proof. It is a trust you can build upon.

Anyone who trusts in [God] will never be put to shame.
Romans 10:11

A man is not justified by observing the law, but by faith in Jesus Christ.

Galatians 2:16

Receive the gift of **Faith** that God has given you. How incredible to realize that your faith in Christ Jesus will result in a life that will last forever!

O Come, All Ye Faithful

O come, all ye faithful, joyful and triumphant,
O come ye, O come ye to Bethlehem;
Come and behold Him, born the King of angels;

Sing, choirs of angels, sing in exultation,
O sing, all ye citizens of heaven above;
Glory to God, all glory in the highest;

Yea, Lord, we greet Thee, born this happy morning,
O Jesus, to Thee be all glory given;
Word of the Father, now in flesh appearing;

Chorus:
O come, let us adore Him, O come, let us adore Him,
O come, let us adore Him, Christ, the Lord. Amen.

In those days Caesar Augustus issued a decree that a census should be taken of the entire Roman world. . . . And everyone went to his own town to register. So Joseph also went from the town of Nazareth in Galilee to Judea, to Bethlehem the town of David, because he belonged to the house and line of David. He went there to register with Mary, who was expecting a child. While they were there, the time came for the baby to be born, and she gave birth to her firstborn, a son. She wrapped him in cloths and placed him in a manger, because there was no room for them in the inn. And there were shepherds living out in the fields nearby, keeping watch over their flocks by night. An angel of the Lord appeared to them, and the glory of the Lord shone around them, and they were terrified. But the angel said to them "Do not be afraid. I bring you good news of great joy that will be for all the people. Today in the town of David a Savior has been born to you; he is Christ the Lord."

Luke 2:1–11

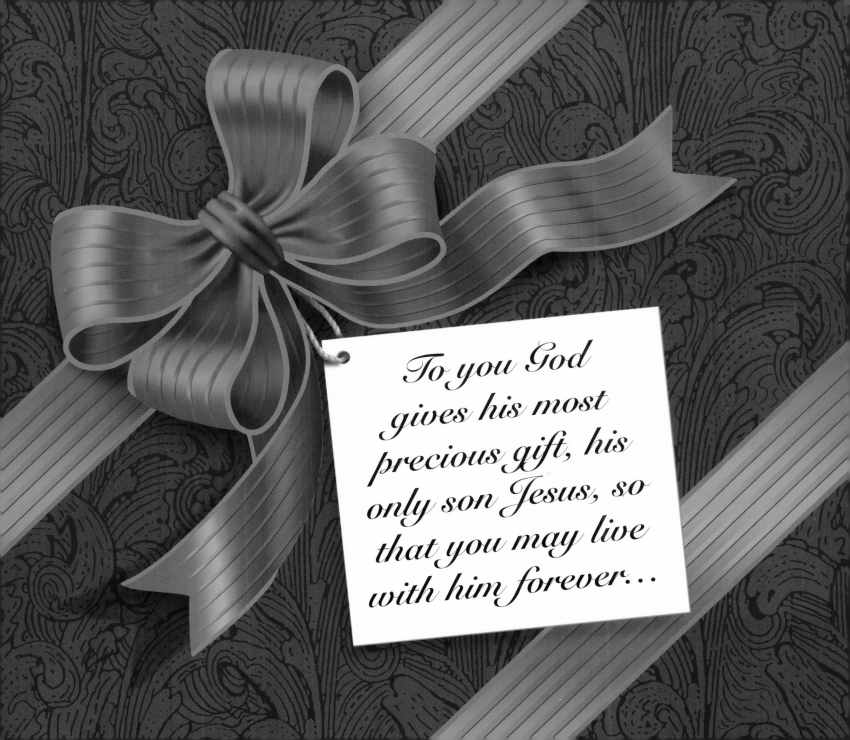

To you God gives his most precious gift, his only son Jesus, so that you may live with him forever…

Experience God's
Christmas Presence!